W9-DDG-461

BEYOND LITTLE WOMEN

A Creative Minds Biography

BEYOND LITTLE WOMEN

A Story about Louisa May Alcott

by Susan Bivin Aller

illustrations by Qi Wang

Carolrhoda Books, Inc./Minneapolis

For Marie-Christine, a treasure in all her roles as daughter-in-law, mother, and friend

Text copyright © 2004 by Susan Bivin Aller
Illustrations copyright © 2004 by Qi Wang

This book is available in two editions:
Library binding by Carolrhoda Books, Inc.,
    a division of Lerner Publishing Group
Soft cover by First Avenue Editions,
    an imprint of Lerner Publishing Group
241 First Avenue North
Minneapolis, MN 55401 U.S.A.

Website address: www.lernerbooks.com

Library of Congress Cataloging-in-Publication Data

Aller, Susan Bivin.
    A story about Louisa May Alcott / by Susan Bivin Aller ; illustrations by
    Qi Wang.
        p.   cm. — (A creative minds biography)
    ISBN: 1–57505–602–X (lib. bdg. : alk. paper)
    ISBN: 1–57505–636–4 (pbk. : alk. paper)
    1. Alcott, Louisa May, 1832–1888—Juvenile literature. 2. Authors,
    American—19th century-Biography—Juvenile literature. I. Wang, Qi.
    II. Title. III. Series.
    PS1018.A45 2004
    813'.4—dc21   2003001305

Manufactured in the United States of America
1 2 3 4 5 6 – JR – 09 08 07 06 05 04

Table of Contents

1

Stuck in the Middle

Four years old today! Little Louisa could scarcely contain her excitement as she skipped along between Mother and her big sister, Anna. They were going to Father's school for a party to celebrate his and Louisa's shared birthday. Bronson Alcott was thirty-seven this day, November 29, 1836.

Louisa—Louy to her family—climbed the steps to the top floor of the Temple School, where Father taught the children of some of Boston's finest families. It was hard for Louy to keep quiet, but she tried. She waited patiently while Father continued his conversation with the pupils.

Finally, it was time for the birthday party. Louy wore a crown of flowers on her head and stood at the teacher's desk to hand out the sweet plummy cakes.

One by one, the children filed by until at last there was only one cake left and one other girl. If Louy gave it to the other girl, she would have none for herself. Oh, how she wanted that plummy cake! She held it close.

Then she heard Mother telling her it was more blessed to give than to receive. Through her tears, Louy gave the cake away. Even on her birthday, Louy had to do something she didn't want to do. It was a hard lesson. What she learned then and never forgot was that she would always have to be a very good girl to get the love and attention she wanted.

Almost from the day she was born—November 29, 1832—Louisa May Alcott had trouble being good. She was a noisy, restless child. Her father, Amos Bronson Alcott, decided that his pretty, vigorous second daughter was a rebel who needed guiding.

The Alcotts' first child, Anna Bronson Alcott, was twenty months older than Louisa. Mild tempered and obedient, Anna was her father's pet. She also had the fair hair and blue eyes of the Alcotts. When Father corrected her for some minor fault, Anna cried and promised to be good so she wouldn't make him unhappy.

Louisa, on the other hand, had the strong will and dark hair and eyes of her mother's family, the Mays.

When Father corrected Louisa, she became even more stubborn. He told her she must learn to control her noisy energy and temper. She tried to become more like Anna, but it was always a struggle. Even Louisa's baby sister, Elizabeth Peabody Alcott, was better at being good and quiet like Anna.

Mother understood Louisa because her middle daughter was so much like herself. Mother came from the wealthy Mays, a Boston family. The Mays were not pleased when their Abigail—called Abba— decided to marry Bronson Alcott. He was only a poor schoolteacher whose uneducated family lived in rural Connecticut. Abba, however, was charmed by the tall, handsome young man and his brilliant theories of education. She hoped he would teach her how to be "womanly." By that she meant controlling her temper and becoming more gentle and submissive. Abba promised that after they were married, she would take care of the practical matters of home and family so Bronson could develop his wonderful ideas.

Since before Louisa was born, Father had been developing his ideas as a schoolteacher. His mother had taught him to write, making the letters with charcoal on the floorboards. When Father grew up, he traveled in the South as a Yankee peddler selling goods from house to house. It was then he formed his original ideas for educating children, and he was quite proud of them.

He believed that children were born with their abilities already inside them and that a teacher's job was to show them how to develop those abilities. He also believed that teachers shouldn't spank or embarrass pupils. Father tried out his theories on his own daughters and kept detailed records of their progress.

Not everyone appreciated Father's theories on education. Parents at his first school in Germantown, Pennsylvania, took their children out of school because of his unusual teaching methods. Father was forced to open a new school in Boston. Twenty-six children attended the Temple School. Father taught his students by reading to them from the Bible or other books and then discussing the stories with them until they agreed with his conclusions.

Mother's life was filled with cooking, laundry, cleaning, and child care. She had little time to give high-quality moral and spiritual guidance to her girls. Father always felt he had superior abilities in moral affairs. He decided to spend more time with his daughters to make up for Mother's shortcomings. He began taking his favorite, Anna, to school with him.

Louisa was stuck in the middle, neither her father's favorite nor her mother's baby. One way she dealt with her frustration was by running away and exploring Boston on her own. Once when she was six, she ran away and found a group of Irish beggar children to play with. They shared their cold potatoes and fish with her. She couldn't find her way home, so that night, she fell asleep on a doorstep. The town crier found her with her head resting on the warm furry shoulder of a Newfoundland dog. The town crier took her to his house and gave her bread and molasses on a tin plate. The next day, Mother tied Louisa to the arm of a sofa with string as punishment.

In 1837 Father published some of his discussions with his students in a book called *Conversations on the Gospels.* It caused a sensation but not the kind Father had hoped for. His openness with his students shocked many people. Soon there were only ten students left in the Temple School.

Father closed the Temple School, and Louisa's family moved into smaller quarters. A few students crowded into the house the Alcotts shared with another family. But even this small school failed when father allowed a black girl to join his class. Even though black people in the North were free, they were not free to attend schools with white children. The parents of Father's remaining students withdrew their children in protest.

Louisa didn't understand all the fuss. The Alcotts had many friends in the antislavery movement. Father and Mother both firmly supported the abolitionists who worked to end slavery in the South. Like her parents, she believed both white and black children should be treated fairly.

Father had no income. He became depressed and angry. "O! What shall I do?" he asked. The answer lay with his friend, the writer Ralph Waldo Emerson. Father and Emerson had become great friends while discussing philosophy. Emerson urged Father to move his family to Concord, the pretty town west of Boston where Emerson lived, and become a philosopher like himself.

Emerson found a small house near his for the Alcotts. He offered to help them pay the rent of fifty-two dollars a year. Father could farm a small piece of land to grow food and could develop his educational theories with Emerson and other philosophers. If the Alcotts needed cash, Father could do odd jobs for neighbors. It sounded like an ideal situation to Father.

Mother, who knew how much her husband disliked physical work of any sort, had doubts about the move. How would they survive? Seven-year-old Louisa, on the other hand, couldn't wait to leave their crowded Boston house and live in the country.

2

Concord: The Happiest Days

In spite of Mother's worries, Concord became—for Louisa, at least—a place of happy events and memories. Dove Cottage was small for a family of five, but its location was perfect for Louisa. Seven-year-old Cyrus Hosmer, the son of the landlord, became Louisa's best friend. They raced, explored the woods, and played near the gentle Concord River that ran behind the house.

"I always thought I must have been a deer or a horse in some former state, because it was such a joy to run," Louisa wrote. "No boy could be my friend until I had beaten him in a race, and no girl if she refused to climb trees, leap fences and be a tomboy."

Concord was a center for New England poets, writers, and philosophers. Louisa knew many of them as neighbors and played with their children. Ralph Waldo Emerson became her friend and allowed her to read books in his library. The naturalist and philosopher Henry David Thoreau lived on Walden Pond nearby. Nathaniel Hawthorne, the famous author, lived down the road.

Emerson and the other neighbors watched with interest as the Alcott family tried to live a life in harmony with nature and the divine spirit. Father and Emerson called this the "transcendental" life. There were no rules to guide them. Father said that by listening for a divine voice inside himself, he would be given the knowledge needed to live honestly.

Just as Mother had feared, Father decided after a few months of digging in his garden and chopping wood for neighbors, that he did not want to soil his hands with work. He felt it was beneath his dignity. He made plans to give philosophical "conversations," asking for voluntary contributions from those who attended. He was sure he could bring in enough money to take care of his family. If not, then he would accept charity.

In the summer of 1840, Louisa's youngest sister was born. Mother and Father named her Abigail May

Alcott, Abby for short. The family, with its four "little women," was complete.

Father taught his girls at home and insisted on their writing something every day. From a young age, Louisa kept a journal. The journal was a way for Louisa and her sisters to practice their writing as well as to reflect on what they had learned that day. The girls left their journals where their parents could read them. Louisa's journal was personal, but she also knew that, like a real author, she had an audience. Often Louisa found comments from Mother or Father in her journal. These were meant to correct or encourage her. "You must help yourself, dear," wrote Mother one day. "The cause of your little troubles is in yourself and patience and courage only will make you what Mother prays to see you—her good and happy girl."

Her journals became a way for Louisa to think about her own troubles and to comment on the people and places around her. They also helped her become a good writer. At the age of eight, Louisa wrote a poem about a robin. Mother compared Louisa to a famous British playwright. "You will grow up a Shakespeare!" she exclaimed. From then on, Mother urged Louisa to write poems and stories in addition to her journal entries.

Louisa's childhood poems were often about nature. One reason was that she and Anna went briefly to a school run by Henry David Thoreau and his brother John. No one in Concord knew more about the woods and hills, the animals and birds than Henry Thoreau. On field trips from school, Thoreau led his class to Walden Pond, where they saw fish swim into his hand and birds come when he whistled. Spiderwebs were fairy handkerchiefs, he told them, and he showed them where to find Indian arrowheads and animal tracks. He opened an enchanted world for Louisa and her classmates. They followed him as if he were a magical Pied Piper.

At home Father grew restless and depressed. His lectures did not make money, and he was angry at the world for not recognizing his genius. Emerson came to the rescue again and paid for Father to go to England, where a group of educators thought Bronson Alcott's theories of education were brilliant. The group had even named a school after him. In May 1842, Father went to England and stayed six months.

Mother found life difficult without her husband, and Anna missed Father very much. But as much as Louisa loved him, she felt happier with Father away. She felt grown up and useful when she could help Mother. Nine-year-old Louisa wished she could do something to earn money. When she was older, she would try.

When Father returned, he brought with him two Englishmen, Henry Wright and Charles Lane, with Lane's young son William. They had come with Father to live a transcendental life and plant a "new heaven on earth" in New England. They would live together in a "consociate family."

Louisa wasn't sure what "consociate" and "transcendental" meant, but she knew the neighbors thought the ideas were very odd. Father explained that they must all live in peace and harmony with nature and each other. He told them that the spirit and mind were more important than the body, so they must think about spiritual things and not worry about money, food, and clothing.

Louisa and her mother couldn't help thinking about the practical side of things. They didn't see how the experiment could work. The "consociate" crowd of nine people who squeezed into the Alcott's small cottage was already making life difficult.

Charles Lane had the money to buy an old farmhouse in Harvard, Massachusetts, not far from Concord. In June 1843, the consociate family moved into the rambling house. They optimistically named it Fruitlands for the orchard they hoped to plant. A few eccentric people came to live the transcendental life with them. One was interested in unusual diets and had lived for a year on nothing but crackers. Another wanted them all to become nudists, although he wore clothes when he was around other people.

The men knew almost nothing about farming. They planned to plow by hand so as not to "exploit" animals. But the work was so hard they gave up and borrowed an ox and a cow—a strange, mismatched team—to pull the plow. They planted wheat, barley, and rye, all mixed together. This grain was central to their survival, since Father decided they could eat no meat.

The Alcotts didn't eat meat because Father said killing animals was wrong. And they couldn't drink milk because he said it robbed calves of their food. They ate only cereal, unleavened bread, fruit, vegetables, and water.

They couldn't wear wool because Father said they shouldn't steal wool from sheep. And they couldn't use cotton because it meant paying planters in the South who used enslaved black people to pick cotton. So they wore smocks made from flax woven into linen.

Mother and the girls did all the cooking, sewing, washing, and other housework.

At first, Louisa enjoyed her new life and the rigid schedules Charles Lane set up for everybody. "I rose at five and had my bath," wrote ten-year-old Louisa that summer. "I love cold water!"

Many times neighbors brought welcome gifts of food or money or wood. The family needed all these things because Father and his friends didn't work. They said working for money was against their higher nature. Yet they gladly accepted gifts other people had worked for.

When the grain was ripe, the men cut and stacked it in the field to dry. Then they left on a trip to New York to lecture on transcendentalism and recruit new members. While they were gone, a thunderstorm blew in. Louisa, Mother, and the other girls struggled to save what they could from the damaging wind and rain. They piled the grain onto bedsheets and dragged it into the barn. Louisa hoped the neighbors would continue to bring them food so they wouldn't starve.

Observers doubted Fruitlands would succeed. "They look well in July," Emerson wrote. "We will see them in December."

By December it was clear that the consociate family would not survive the winter on their harsh life and poor diet. One evening Mother and Father sat Anna and Louisa down for a long talk.

They discussed moving to a nearby Shaker community where the men and women lived separately. Louisa cried herself to sleep one night. She feared her own faults were causing the problems. "I wish I was rich, I was good, and we were all a happy family," she wrote in her journal.

A month later, the consociate family admitted defeat. Charles Lane and his son went to live with the Shakers, and the Alcotts moved to rented rooms in Still River, Massachusetts. Father fell into a deep depression at the failure of his grand experiment. Mother took complete charge of the family's affairs.

Louisa, twelve and at the beginning of adolescence, saw how much her mother had sacrificed to be a good wife to Father. Louisa was determined to be independent when she grew up and never allow herself to need anything from someone else. She would earn her own way in the world.

3

The Pathetic Family

A year later, Mother bought a house in Concord using a gift from Emerson and money she had inherited from her father. The house was called Hillside. Father was glad to return to Concord where his friends Emerson and Thoreau lived. He made himself useful by repairing and adding on to the old, rundown house. He and Mother talked of starting another transcendental Eden, this time at Hillside. They invited Father's emotionally unstable brother, Junius, to come live with them. An orphaned teenage boy and a middle-aged single female schoolteacher also came.

Louisa complained in her journal, "I wish we could be together, and no one else. I don't see who is to clothe and feed us all, when we are so poor now."

Charles Lane also returned, to Louisa's annoyance. He came back to spend the summer and reestablished his strict routine for the family. He continually quizzed Louisa and Anna about their faults, asking questions like "What vices do you wish less of?" Louisa, with some sarcasm, listed idleness, activity, impudence, and love of cats.

Tall, slim Louisa, with her dark hair and sparkling eyes, had a great sense of fun, lots of energy, and plenty of daring. In the barn at Hillside, Louisa, her sisters, and their friends set up a stage and produced amateur plays. Louisa usually wrote the lively scripts. Then, dressed in shawls, satin slippers, old curtains, and other finery from their attics, the children acted out Louisa's stories of knights, bandits, witches, and magicians. Theater gave Louisa a safe way to express all the strong emotions that her parents told her she must control.

It was at Hillside that Louisa saw slavery with a human face for the first time. The Alcotts sheltered a man who had just escaped from his master in the South and was on his way to freedom in Canada. Louisa was deeply moved by the slave's tale of suffering and his fears for his future.

When Louisa was thirteen, her parents gave her something she wanted very much. "I have at last got the little room I have wanted so long," she wrote in her journal. "It does me good to be alone. . . . The door that opens into the garden will be very pretty in summer, and I can run off to the woods when I like."

At fifteen Louisa opened a school in the barn. Her pupils were three of Emerson's children, Waldo, Ellen, and Edith. She taught them what she knew of reading, arithmetic, and nature. For her favorite, eleven-year-old Ellen, Louisa wrote fairy tales about flowers and woodland creatures. Just as Henry Thoreau had led Louisa into an enchanted world, Louisa led Ellen Emerson. Louisa bound these "flower fables" into tiny books for Ellen.

Father still had no regular work. Instead, he chopped wood and did odd jobs for Emerson and others. Friends and family gave the Alcotts some charitable gifts, but they were not enough. Mother tried to make money any way she could. For a few months she was paid to care for a mentally handicapped teenage girl in their house. In the summer, she worked herself to exhaustion as matron in a spa in Maine. Mother hoped Anna, Louisa, and Elizabeth were old enough to help by earning money too. Could Louisa paint decorative ornaments to sell? Maybe they could open a small school where Anna could teach German and Elizabeth could teach piano.

As Louisa entered adolescence, she took on the role of being the strongest member of her family next to her mother. She vowed "to do something, by and by—don't care what—teach, sew, act, write, anything to help the family; and I'll be rich and famous and happy before I die, see if I won't."

All too soon for Louisa, the Hillside days ended. Louisa didn't want to leave the calm and beauty of Concord, where she had friends and her special room to write in. But her mother was desperate. In November 1848, when Louisa turned sixteen, the Alcotts rented out Hillside and moved to Boston. Mother could think of no way to earn enough money in Concord, but in Boston, she had friends and relatives who might help. The family rented cramped rooms in Boston's South End. Father gave "conversations" on transcendentalism near the bookshop of his former teaching assistant, Elizabeth Peabody. When there was no audience, he would sit in her bookshop and read the journals he couldn't afford to buy.

Boston was crowded with new immigrants and others who needed homes, jobs, and food. Mother had grown up in a family that had great sympathy for the poor, so when a group of her wealthy Boston friends offered her a job as a missionary to the city's poor, she accepted. She thus became one of America's first social workers, handing out food and clothing, Bibles, and religious tracts. She also found housekeeping work for unemployed women.

Louisa and Anna helped as much as they could. Anna worked for a few months as a governess. She was so gloomy and unhappy to be away from her own family that her employers were actually glad when she quit. Louisa also worked briefly, as a companion to an invalid. She felt degraded by the heavy, dirty chores, and she returned home as well. Father and Mother felt their daughters were above doing such menial work and praised them for being noble and unwilling to bow to the will of others.

Writing was becoming Louisa's most satisfying work. She still kept an open journal that her parents could read and comment in. But she hoped for a larger audience and began sending poems and stories to magazines. At nineteen Louisa's first published work appeared in a popular women's magazine. It was a poem called "Sunlight." Later that year, she sold her first short story to a Christian magazine.

When she was twenty, she breezed confidently into the Boston office of James T. Fields with a manuscript in hand. Fields was a bookseller who knew the Alcott family and had published books by Emerson,

Hawthorne, and Thoreau. Louisa had written a story fictionalizing her recent unhappy experience as a companion to the invalid. Fields turned her down flat. "Stick to your teaching, Miss Alcott," he told her, with a twinkle in his eye. "You can't write."

Well, she would show him!

Eventually, Louisa did find a publisher. He agreed to print *Flower Fables,* the stories she had told to Emerson's daughter Ellen. Looking at the beautiful little illustrated book when it was published in 1855, Louisa said she felt as proud as a new mother with her firstborn child. More stories flowed from Louisa's pen, and she sold them to magazine publishers, who began to recognize the young author's name and eagerly wait for her next stories. Writing was to be her life's work. She was certain of that. Income from her published stories helped pay the family's bills. And the stories, like her plays, were an important out-let for the dramatic extremes of her emotions.

In the summer of 1855, the Alcotts accepted an invitation from cousins to live rent free in Walpole, New Hampshire. Charity again! Louisa, who saw the humor in their situation, referred to the Alcotts as "the pathetic family." She came to think of her parents as grown-up children who had little control over their lives.

Louisa reveled in the beautiful hills and woods of New Hampshire. She felt alive again after living in cramped rooms in noisy, crowded Boston. In her journal, she recorded the joys of carefree days with young friends. She and Anna joined an amateur theater company. Anna was a fine actress and often played the leading roles. Louisa, on the other hand, was more suited to tragedy, melodrama, or comedy. She was tall, with a well-formed body, flashing dark eyes, and thick, chestnut hair. At social gatherings, Louisa often performed one of the humorous monologues she had written.

As much as she loved her family, Louisa desperately needed to be away from their constant demands on her if she was ever to do serious writing. She went to Boston alone that November and lived with a close family friend. She would never be lonely in Boston with so many entertainments and many friends and family members living there. And in Boston, she could have her independence. "I can't do much with my hands," she wrote her father, "so I will make a battering ram of my head and make a way through this rough and tumble world."

In the spring, Louisa returned to spend the summer with her family in New Hampshire. She was shocked at what she found. Elizabeth and Abby had caught scarlet fever from neighbors their mother had nursed. Although Abby recovered, Elizabeth became weaker and more frail. In spite of all her family and the doctors could do, Elizabeth was slowly fading away. For the next two years, Louisa worked and wrote in Boston, but she returned periodically to help the family care for her dying sister. Louisa and Mother sat at Elizabeth's bedside when she died in March 1858 at the age of twenty-two. Mother felt guilty for the rest of her life. "I dare not dwell on the fever which I carried to my home," she wrote.

Another break soon came as well. Anna, twenty-seven, became engaged to John Pratt, a longtime friend and neighbor. Although Anna delayed her marriage two years out of respect for Elizabeth's death, she would leave the family circle to devote her life to John Pratt. Louisa knew that young Abby, who always got her own way, would also leave one day. Abby would never give up her artistic ambitions for the needs of the family.

Louisa saw clearly that she was the only daughter able to take responsibility for her dependent parents. Little four-year-old Louy, who once gave up her plummy cake to another, had learned her lesson well. Grown-up Louisa was prepared to make costly sacrifices for her family.

4

Orchard House

A few months after Elizabeth's death, Louisa and her family returned to Concord and moved into Orchard House. Mother had bought it with money inherited from her father. A path separated the house from Hillside, the house that held such happy memories for Louisa. The author Nathaniel Hawthorne owned that house and had changed its name to Wayside.

Orchard House was a rundown farmhouse on ten acres of land. There was plenty of wood to cut for winter fires, room for vegetable gardens, and forty apple trees. Louisa called it "Apple Slump" after a favorite family dessert. Father and the girls set about at once to repair and decorate the house. Eighteen-year-old Abby painted bright birds, flowers, and angels on walls.

The Alcott's were glad to be back among old friends in Concord, especially Father, who found inspiration in the company of Emerson. Soon the Alcotts were holding open house for their friends every Monday evening. As Abby played the old piano, they sang, danced, and played games. Sometimes Louisa entertained by telling her scary ghost stories. Afterward, Mother served root beer, gingerbread, and the celebrated apple slump.

As life in Orchard House settled into a comfortable routine, Father made plans for a "conversational tour" to the West to earn money by lecturing about his philosophical ideas. Louisa went back to Boston for the winter to be the family breadwinner again. She found work as governess to Alice Lovering, an invalid girl she had once tutored. The job paid well and allowed time off in the evenings to write. Louisa sent money home to pay for clothes for her sisters, art lessons for Abby, and comforts for Orchard House.

Louisa went home to Concord again in the spring of 1859. She found the sleepy town in turmoil over fears that a war to end slavery in the South was coming soon. More and more, Louisa longed to do something active in the fight to free slaves.

At twenty-eight, Louisa had developed into a handsome woman with passionate feelings and strong opinions. Father's insistence that she try to control these emotions and become more passive and "feminine" angered and frustrated Louisa. If she had to repress her true feelings in everyday life, then she would have to unleash them somewhere else.

She decided to write a novel. She wanted to leave the world of fairy tales and magazine articles and make a name for herself in the world of adult fiction. When Louisa was captured by an idea, she wrote almost nonstop for days. She called this "going into her vortex." It was like being held in the center of a whirl of ideas that she couldn't escape until the work was finished. In 1861 Louisa entered her vortex to write a novel she called *Moods*. For four weeks, she wrote all day and into the night. Father and Mother took her cups of tea and apples but didn't break her concentration. At the end of four weeks, Louisa put down her pen, utterly exhausted, and set aside her completed novel to "settle" until she could read and edit it with a fresh eye.

These tremendous bursts of writing, followed by physical collapse, became Louisa's typical pattern. In winter, when her Orchard House bedroom was cold, she wore an old red and green party wrap—her "glory cloak"—and kept her head warm with a green silk cap with a red bow that Mother had made.

Louisa's ideas for stories grew more varied as she developed her writing skills. She entered a publisher's contest with a story called *Pauline's Passion and Punishment.* It was the first of what Louisa called her "lurid" or "blood and thunder" thrillers. Her story won the contest, and she was paid one hundred dollars. This encouraged her to write more, which the publisher gladly bought. She didn't want her family and friends to know she was writing these stories of women's revenge, anger, and violence—so different from her other work. So she published them under a made-up name, "A. M. Barnard."

In the spring of 1861, the war between the North and South began in earnest. Louisa saw young men in Boston and Concord going away to fight. She and the other women stayed home to sew and make bandages. She wished she were a man and could join the battle. Then Dorothea Dix, the country's supervisor of nurses, issued a call for nurses. After years of caring for her family and others, Louisa felt sure she qualified. She enlisted and was assigned to Washington, D.C., and the dismal Union Hotel, which had been converted into a hospital.

Louisa had no idea what she was getting into. She vaguely imagined a sort of home nursing on a large scale. Thinking about her patients' comfort, she took with her a teakettle and books by popular British author Charles Dickens. But the reality was grim. When she reported for work in December 1862, her first job was to strip and bathe the muddy, blood-stained soldiers as they were brought in from the battlefields.

For a genteel, unmarried woman of thirty, this was a shocking experience. Conditions in the hospital were appalling. Putrid air, the terrible stench of wounds and illness, and the lack of sanitation made many of the wounded and staff ill. Louisa worked from six in the morning until nine at night, dressing the men's wounds, running for bed linens, water, and other essentials. She fed the men who couldn't do it themselves and wrote letters for them.

After only three weeks, Louisa fell ill herself. The doctors diagnosed typhoid pneumonia and dosed her with calomel, a medicine made with mercury. Large doses of calomel brought about mercury poisoning that sometimes killed patients instead of curing them. At the very least, as with Louisa, calomel caused hair loss, a swollen tongue, loss of voice, and sore gums.

Louisa lay dangerously ill and delirious. When she woke, she saw Father by her bedside. The hospital had sent for him. He took Louisa home to Orchard House.

At home Louisa suffered nightmares and strange visions and caused much alarm to her parents and Abby, who took turns nursing her. The pain that remained in her mouth was so great that her doctor prescribed heavy drugs for sleep. More than two months passed before Louisa was well enough to leave her room. For the rest of her life, she suffered the painful effects of mercury poisoning in her body.

When her health improved, a magazine editor asked her to write about her hospital experiences. From her vivid memories of those weeks, she wrote a series of articles called *Hospital Sketches*. Readers couldn't wait for the next article to appear. Soon she received several offers to publish the articles as a book. The book brought a flood of letters from readers and praise from reviewers. It quickly sold out, and more copies were printed. The lesson to Louisa was clear. Writing from her own experience, about things she knew, was going to be the key to her success as a writer.

Partly because of the success of *Hospital Sketches* and partly because she was becoming a recognized name to magazine readers, Louisa was being asked by more and more publishers to write stories for their magazines. She had spent years "sitting in a corner," she said, and working unnoticed like poor Cinderella.

Her sudden success was a sweet victory.

In October Louisa paid for art lessons in Boston for talented Abby—who suddenly announced that she wished to be called "May" to distinguish herself from her mother, Abba. May wanted independence, and she always got her own way. While Louisa was somewhat envious, she gladly supported May and paid for her studies. She even made clothes for the charming blonde girl. Louisa, with her dark good looks, loved fashionable clothes and luxuries too, but she didn't have the nerve to cross Father. He thought all such vanities should be avoided.

Whenever Louisa went back to Orchard House from Boston, she wrote story after story in her own room. However, she often had to stop for weeks at a time to nurse Mother or Anna. Mother was becoming old and frail, and Anna often fell ill. Anna, her husband, and their new baby had moved back to Orchard House because Anna was always homesick when she was away from her own family. During those hard times, after caring for her family and the house, Louisa had no energy left for her writing. Eventually, she realized she was earning enough money as a writer to hire a maid. But the maid caught typhoid fever, and Louisa ended up nursing her for six weeks and resuming all the housework too.

The best news of the year was the publication in December 1864 of Louisa's novel *Moods.* She had rewritten it several times and finally found a publisher for it. One reviewer compared her first published novel to the works of Nathaniel Hawthorne, Louisa's admired friend and neighbor. At the same time, Louisa's secret identity as A. M. Barnard brought pleasure and a good income to her as well. The readers of her "lurid tales" were eager for more of her work.

The year 1865 offered Louisa another pleasure, the promise of a trip abroad. Louisa had longed to visit Europe but knew she could never afford travel expenses. The opportunity came from the Weld family in Boston, who wanted to pay Louisa to accompany their twenty-nine-year-old invalid daughter, Anna, on a grand tour of Europe. Louisa was afraid her family could not get along without her, but they convinced her that she should go. The ship sailed in July, with Louisa taking responsibility for the fussy Anna Weld.

Except for a few times, Louisa's year abroad didn't come close to her dream of a vacation in Europe. The trip was dampened by the fretful and spoiled Anna Weld and often by her own poor health. Even so, in England, Belgium, Germany, and Italy she filled her head with enough pictures of Europe to last her life.

The touring finally became too much for Louisa, and she left Anna Weld in the care of a nurse and companion. Then she spent two happy weeks in Paris with Ladislas "Laddie" Wisniewski. She and Anna Weld had met the charming eighteen-year-old Polish man in Switzerland. Louisa and Laddie took walks together and enjoyed the French city in each other's company. Finally, Louisa spent several weeks in London before returning to her family, exactly one year after she left them.

As she feared, the "pathetic family" had fallen into debt without her. Orchard House needed repairs, her sister Anna was growing deaf, and Mother was becoming blind and senile. Once more, Louisa took responsibility for them all. The stress brought on joint and muscle pains and blinding headaches, a flair up of mercury poisoning. Even so, she wrote twelve stories in six months, including another of A. M. Barnard's "lurid tales."

In September a magazine publisher offered her the editorship of a children's magazine called *Merry's Museum.* At the same time, Thomas Niles, publisher of *Hospital Sketches,* asked her to write a book for girls about a real-life family to compete with the popular boys' books by Oliver Optic.

Louisa wasn't sure she wanted to write for children. But she needed to support her family, and these were good offers. She said yes to editing *Merry's Museum.* Then she sat down at the writing table in her Orchard House bedroom and began to think about the four sisters—the little women—of her own family. This was certainly a real-life story she knew well. Could she make a successful book from the stories of their childhood?

5

Reliving Childhood

Louisa entered her vortex and began to write a fictional story based on her memories of growing up. She and her sisters became the "little women" of the March family. Louisa, of course, was strong, practical Jo. Her older sister Anna became beautiful, competent Meg. Elizabeth, who died tragically young, was wise little Beth. And May, with her artistic abilities and fancy ways, became Amy.

In the story's opening lines, Louisa captured all their personalities:

> "Christmas won't be Christmas without any presents," grumbled Jo, lying on the rug.
>
> "It's so dreadful to be poor!" sighed Meg, looking down at her old dress.
>
> "I don't think it's fair for some girls to have plenty of pretty things, and other girls nothing at all," added little Amy, with an injured sniff.
>
> "We've got father and mother and each other," said Beth, contentedly, from her corner.

Louisa knew that Mother was the ideal model for Marmee, the mother of the March sisters. Father, however, was not typical of the fathers most families had. So in her book, Louisa sent Mr. March away to war as a chaplain, where he could be loved from afar but not often seen.

She drew other characters in the book from her friends, neighbors, and people she had met. Laurie, the boy next door, for example, was in part drawn from Louisa's memory of the young Polish man Laddie whom she had met in Europe.

It took Louisa less than three months to write the 402 pages of *Little Women.* She had learned to write quickly, out of need to finish stories and get paid for them.

Little Women came out in September 1868. Girls all over the country fell in love with the March family. For the first time, someone had written a book about a family that spoke and acted the way real families did. Louisa's memory of the Alcott childhood at Hillside and Orchard House held enough material for several books. Schools, parties, money troubles, illness, holidays, friends—all had poured from Louisa's memory into the book. And there was no need to tag on moral lessons to her stories the way most children's books did at the time. The basic goodness, humor, and optimism of the Alcotts glowed on every page.

The success of *Little Women* surprised Louisa with a fame she did not expect, although she found it pleasant enough. She joked that people were coming to stare at the Alcotts. Sometimes she dressed as a servant when opening the door to strangers and said Miss Alcott was not at home.

The reading public clamored for more books by Miss Alcott. Her publisher urged her to write another book for girls. Louisa gave in to his demands, writing *An Old-Fashioned Girl* in 1870. Another book meant more financial security for her family.

May took her first trip to Europe that same year, paid for by a friend. She took Louisa with her. This time Louisa paid her own way. No longer was she dependent on other people to give her the luxuries she desired. She was, in fact, becoming quite wealthy and was making wise investments in the stock market.

Seven months into the tour, news came to them that Anna's husband, John Pratt, had died at the age of thirty-seven. He left behind his wife and two sons, with no income for them. Louisa knew that she would never be able to travel this far away from her family again. For the rest of her life, she would be their only support.

During the last precious months of freedom, while staying in Rome, Louisa wrote *Little Men.* The novel became a story about Plumfield, a boys' school run by a grown-up Jo March and her husband. Louisa poured into it her childhood memories of teachers and the adventures of the schoolrooms. She wrote it as a tribute to John Pratt and to her nephews, Fred and John.

Louisa returned to the United States on June 6, 1871, the day *Little Men* was published. Father and her publisher met her at the ship carrying an advertising banner for the book.

During the next years, Louisa returned to her

longtime pattern of living in Boston and returning to Concord when her family needed her. She also became a vocal supporter of women's right to vote and other reforms. As the famous children's author Miss Louisa May Alcott, she was often asked to give her opinion on a variety of important issues. And she certainly had her strong opinions.

In 1875 she attended the historic Women's Congress in Syracuse, New York. At this gathering, women from all over the country discussed such topics as women's rights as citizens and women in art and culture. Louisa went simply as an observer, but she was recognized. Crowds of women pressed around the popular author, asking Louisa for autographs or kisses.

Louisa continued her series of children's novels with *Eight Cousins* in 1875, followed by its sequel *Rose in Bloom* the next year. Her public was delighted, but she was growing tired of providing, as she put it, moral pap for the young. She relieved her weariness as she had done other times: she went to a hotel in Boston and wrote a sensational novel. *A Modern Mephistopheles* is filled with scenes of corruption, drugs, and forbidden love. It was published anonymously. Louisa May Alcott would never dare to write such a story under her own name!

May returned to Europe to continue her art studies in September 1876. She was happier abroad where she could be around other artists and where her paintings won praise from critics. But Mother was very upset by May's departure. Mother had been visibly failing for several years, and she felt the end was near.

Nurse Louisa remained on duty, while Anna kept house. Finally, in November 1877, Mother died peacefully in Louisa's arms. A few days later, on November 29, Louisa and Father silently observed their forty-fifth and seventy-eighth birthdays together. Louisa grieved for Mother, whose life had been so intertwined with her own. She wrote to May that she was quite ready to die herself, since Mother no longer needed her. Father and Louisa both felt lost and without purpose in life.

May wrote from Europe that she had fallen in love with Ernest Nieriker, a young Swiss banker. They planned to be married in March. She never wanted to return to America. Life in Europe was exciting and glamorous and the best place to pursue her artistic career. She hoped Louisa would come to visit in the fall and see for herself.

Meanwhile, Father reached the high point of his career when he helped to form the Concord School of Philosophy. As dean of the new school, Father had an eager audience for all the subjects he cherished. The downside for Louisa and Anna was that they were expected to run a sort of hotel at Orchard House for the budding philosophers. "They roost on our steps," Louisa complained, "like hens waiting for corn." Still, Bronson's daughters were proud of their father, the good old gray-haired philosopher who seemed happy and fulfilled at last.

May—Mrs. Ernest Nieriker—wrote from Paris that she was expecting a baby in November. Louisa planned to go and be with her, but poor health held her back. She sent baby clothes instead and rejoiced with Father and Anna when news came of the birth of May's daughter. She was named Louisa May Nieriker and called Lulu.

The Alcotts' joy was short-lived. May became ill with meningitis and died on December 29. With her husband's permission, she had named Louisa their baby's guardian.

6

The Hard-Earned Harvest

Father had once written a poem to Louisa, expressing his love for her and his understanding that she had lived a life of sacrifice for her family. He concluded by writing, "I press thee to my heart as Duty's faithful child." That praise from Father was long in coming. It had often seemed to Louisa that she could never please him, no matter how much she tried.

Louisa, who already took responsibility for her father and Anna's family, prepared to become guardian and mother to tiny Lulu, who was being brought to America by Ernest Nieriker's teenage sister and a nurse. Lulu would arrive in September 1880, when she was just ten months old. Louisa was nearly forty-eight.

Suddenly into the Alcotts' lives came a merry, blonde, blue-eyed baby. The captain carried her from the ship, and she reached out her tiny arms to Louisa, saying "Marmar." The child brought joy to the family who was still grieving over the death of May. Louisa fluttered about, hiring and firing nursemaids, entertaining people who came to see "Miss Alcott's baby," and trying to keep on with her writing.

She could have retired from writing and still earned a large income from the sales of her books and from her investments. She was living her childhood dream of becoming rich and famous, but she also had become a woman for whom writing was as essential as breathing. She told stories to Lulu, and they became *Lulu's Library.* Other short pieces became *Aunt Jo's Scrapbag, Shawl Straps,* and *Spinning Wheel Stories.*

She wrote a sequel to *Little Men,* called *Jo's Boys,* slowly and with difficulty. Midway through writing it, as she struggled with her own ill health, Father suffered a paralyzing stroke. In the months that followed, Louisa juggled her duties as nurse to Father, mother to

Lulu, and author. Although no one expected Father to live long after his stroke, the hardy old man survived in a feeble state for five and a half more years.

Louisa bought a summerhouse on the Massachusetts shore at Nonquitt and found some peace there with little Lulu, Anna, and her grown nephews. Finally, her body and nerves broke under the stress of work and the effects of mercury poisoning from her Civil War days. She had great difficulty walking, she had rheumatic pains, stomach and liver problems, terrible headaches, dizziness, and nightmares. She tried many kinds of treatments, including magnetism and mind cures. She moved into a nursing home in Roxbury, near Boston, under the care of her kind friend and doctor, Rhoda Lawrence.

She faced her last months bravely and with her usual practical good sense. She adopted Anna's son, John Pratt, so he could renew the copyrights on her books and handle her legal affairs. She reread old letters and journals and destroyed many she considered too personal for other people to read. When she could no longer write, she kept her hands busy with sewing clothes for poor children.

Louisa went to see her father for the last time on March 1, 1888. He was very weak but also peaceful. Father's last words to Louisa were "I am going up.

Come soon." He died three days later. With Father at peace and no longer dependent on her, Louisa gave up her own fight to keep her tortured body alive. She complained of a searing headache and not long afterward lapsed into a coma. On March 6, at the age of fifty-five, Louisa followed him "up."

Louisa May Alcott's great courage, generosity, and love remained with her until the end of her life. Not long before she died, she wrote a poem called "My Prayer." In it she asked for courage and patience to bear her pain. And she expressed a longing to share with others "the hard-earned harvest of these years."

More than one hundred years after her death, stories by Louisa May Alcott are still read and loved around the world. It is a rich harvest indeed.

Further Reading, Films, and Websites

Books in Print by Louisa May Alcott
1855 *Flower Fables*
1863 *Hospital Sketches*
1864 *Moods*
1868 *Little Women*
1869 *Good Wives: Little Women Part II*
1870 *An Old-Fashioned Girl*
1871 *Little Men*
1873 *Transcendental Wild Oats*
1873 *Work: A Story of Experience*
1875 *Eight Cousins*
1876 *Rose in Bloom*
1878 *Under the Lilacs*
1880 *Jack and Jill: A Village Story*
1886 *Jo's Boys and How They Turned Out: A Sequal to*
  Little Men
1886–1889 *Lulu's Library*
2001 *The Girlhood Diary of Louisa May Alcott*

Films Based on Books by Louisa May Alcott
1997 *Little Men*
1933 and 1994 *Little Women*

Websites about Louisa May Alcott
Orchard House
  <http://www.louisamayalcott.org>

Bibliography

Alcott, Louisa May. *Hospital Sketches.* Chester, CT: Applewood Books, 1993.

Alcott, Louisa May. *Jo's Boys.* Boston: Little, Brown & Co., 1994.

Alcott, Louisa May. *The Journals of Louisa May Alcott.* Eds. Joel Meyerson, Daniel Shealy, with assistance of Madeleine B. Stern. Boston: Little, Brown & Co., 1989.

Alcott, Louisa May. *Little Women.* New York: Viking, 1997.

Alcott, Louisa May. *Louisa May Alcott: Life, Letters, and Journals.* Edited by Ednah D. Cheney. New York: Random House, 1995.

Alcott, Louisa May. *An Old-Fashioned Girl.* Boston: Little, Brown & Co., 1997.

Alcott, Louisa May. "Recollections of My Childhood," *The Youth's Companion,* May 24, 1888.

Alcott, Louisa May. *Rose in Bloom.* Boston: Little, Brown & Co., 1995.

Anderson, William. *The World of Louisa May Alcott.* New York: HarperCollins, 1992.

Anthony, Katherine. *Louisa May Alcott.* New York: Alfred A. Knopf, 1938.

Gowing, Clara. *The Alcotts as I Knew Them.* Boston: C. M. Clark, 1909.

Johnston, Norma. *Louisa May: The World and Work of Louisa May Alcott.* New York: Maxwell Macmillan Inc., 1991.

Meigs, Cornelia. *Invincible Louisa: The Story of the Author of* Little Women. Boston: Little, Brown & Co., 1933.

Saxton, Martha. *Louisa May: A Modern Biography of Louisa May Alcott.* Boston: Houghton Mifflin, 1977.

Stern, Madeleine B. *Louisa May Alcott: A Biography.* Boston: Northeastern University Press, 1996.

All quotations in this biography were taken from the above sources.

Index